THE
CHICAGO
BEARS

Jamie Fickett

THE
GREEN BAY
PACKERS

A Stingray Book

SEAHORSE
PUBLISHING

Teaching Tips for Caregivers and Teachers:

This Hi-Lo book features high-interest subject matter that will appeal to all readers in intermediate and middle school grades. It may be enjoyed by students reading at or above grade level as well as by those who are looking for age-appropriate themes matched with a less challenging reading level. Hi-Lo books are ideal for ELL readers, too.

Each book appeals to a striving reader's age and maturity level. Opportunities are provided for students to read words they already know while encountering a limited number of new, high-interest vocabulary words. With these supports in place, students will read more fluently while increasing reading comprehension. Use the following suggestions to help students grow as readers.

- Encourage the student to read independently at home.
- Encourage the student to practice reading aloud.
- Encourage activities that require reading.
- Establish a regular reading time.
- Have the student write questions about what they read.

Teaching Tips for Teachers:

Before Reading

- Ask, "What do I know about this topic?"
- Ask, "What do I want to learn about this topic?"

During Reading

- Ask, "What is the author trying to teach me?"
- Ask, "How is this like something I already know?"

After Reading

- Discuss how the text features (headings, index, etc.) help with understanding the topic.
- Ask, "What interesting or fun fact did you learn?"

TABLE OF CONTENTS

GRIDIRON GREATS

The Green Bay Packers and the Chicago Bears have the oldest **rivalry** in the history of the NFL (National Football League).

Games between the Packers and the Bears are always some of the best matchups in sports.

The teams combined have 22 NFL Championships and 58 players in the Pro Football Hall of Fame.

FUN FACT

It takes about three hours to drive between Chicago, Illinois, and Green Bay, Wisconsin.

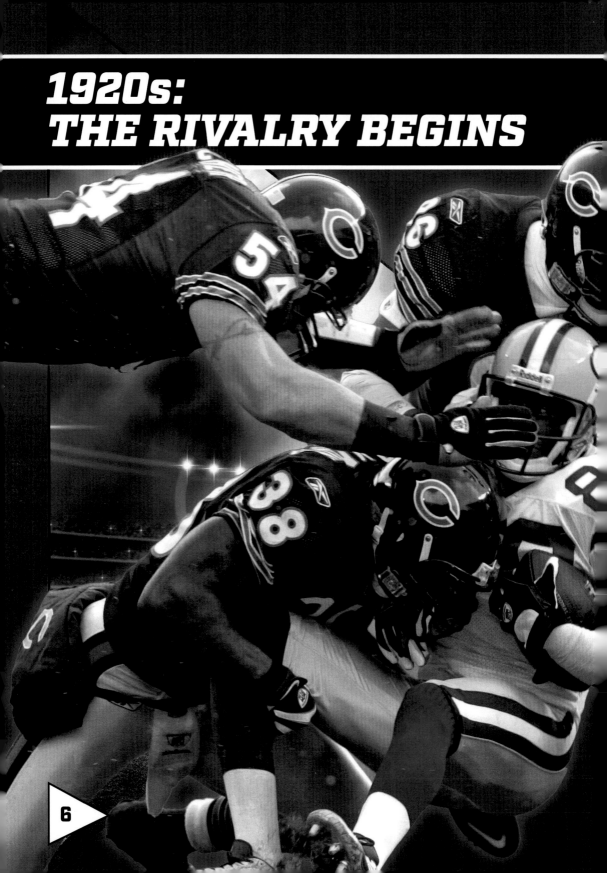

1920s:
THE RIVALRY BEGINS

The teams first played in 1921. At the time, the team from Illinois was called the Staleys. The Staleys beat the Packers 20 to 0.

In a 1924 game, Bears player Frank Hanny and Packers player Tillie Voss threw punches. They were the first players in NFL history to get **ejected** for fighting. The Bears won 3 to 0.

FUN FACT

In 1922, the Chicago Staleys changed their name to the Chicago Bears.

1941: REVENGE

The Bears were undefeated for the season. They had outscored their opponents by 157 points.

Then, on November 2, 1941, the Packers shocked the country with a 16 to 14 win over Chicago.

But the Bears got their revenge. They beat Green Bay in the **playoffs** and won the 1941 NFL Championship.

On November 12, 1961, legendary NFL coach Vince Lombardi took the Packers to a 31 to 7 lead over Chicago.

The Bears came back to score three touchdowns with the help of **rookie** Mike Ditka. It wasn't enough. The Packers won 31 to 28.

Later that year, Green Bay was crowned NFL Champion.

FUN FACT

The Super Bowl Lombardi Trophy is named after coach Vince Lombardi.

The Bears and the Packers faced off on November 17, 1963.

Both teams had an 8 and 1 record. Both teams were tied for first place in the National Football Conference.

The Bears defense held the Packers to 7 points. Chicago won 26 to 7.

The Bears went on to win the 1963 NFL Championship.

FUN FACT

The NFC (National Football Conference) and the AFC (American Football Conference) make up the NFL.

The Bears **dominated** the rivalry for much of the 1980s.

It started on December 7, 1980. Famed running back Walter Payton ran all over the Packers defense. He scored three touchdowns and led the Bears to a 61 to 7 victory.

The undefeated Bears beat the Packers 23 to 7 on October 21, 1985. Star tackle William "The Refrigerator" Perry scored the touchdown that gave Chicago the lead.

FUN FACT

Many people claim that the 1985 Chicago Bears were one of the best NFL teams of all time.

1989: UNDER REVIEW

On November 5, 1989, the Bears winning streak over the Packers came to an end. Green Bay beat them in a **controversial** game.

In the fourth quarter, a touchdown pass to Packers wide receiver Sterling Sharpe went under review.

Green Bay won 14 to 13.

FUN FACT

The Packers beat the Chicago Bears 12 times between 1992 and 1998.

17

1999: UPSET

The game against the Packers on November 7, 1999, was emotional for the Bears. Beloved Chicago running back Walter Payton had just passed away.

Playing in Green Bay, the Bears **upset** the Packers. They blocked a 28-yard **field goal** with just seconds left in the game.

FUN FACT

Walter Payton got the nickname "Sweetness" after he yelled, "Your sweetness is your weakness!" to a defender.

THE RIVALRY CONTINUES

Today's talented players continue the **epic** rivalry between the Chicago Bears and the Green Bay Packers.

Chicago quarterback Justin Fields matches up against the Green Bay star defense led by cornerback Jaire Alexander and linebacker De'Vondre Campbell.

Who will win the next battle between these two great teams?

FUN FACT

Green Bay beat the Bears twice in the 2023–2024 season, earning them a spot in the NFL playoffs.

GLOSSARY

controversial (kahn-truh-VUR-shuhl): causing a great deal of disagreement

dominated (DAH-muh-nay-ted): controlled or ruled

ejected (i-JEK-tid): removed from a game

epic (EP-ik): amazing or impressive

field goal (feeld gohl): a play in which the ball is kicked from the field, through the goalposts, scoring three points

playoffs (PLAY-awfs): games after the regular season that determine which teams will compete for the championship

rivalry (RYE-vuhl-ree): a longstanding, competitive, up-and-down relationship between two teams

rookie (RUK-ee): a professional athlete in their first season of play

upset (uhp-SET): to defeat unexpectedly

INDEX

AFTER READING QUESTIONS

1. How did Frank Hanny and Tillie Voss make history in a 1924 game?

2. What was controversial about a 1989 game between the rivals?

3. What was the original team name of the Chicago Bears?

4. Which team dominated the rivalry in the 1980s?

5. How many members of the Pro Football Hall of Fame do the two teams have combined?

ABOUT THE AUTHOR

Jamie Fickett lives in Long Island, New York. He enjoys sports, especially baseball. He likes to go to Mets games to watch his favorite player, Pete Alonso, play. He also enjoys cooking his famous chili and watching Formula 1 racing.

Written by: Jamie Fickett
Design by: Kathy Walsh
Editor: Kim Thompson

Library of Congress PCN Data
The Chicago Bears vs. The Green Bay Packers
/Jamie Fickett
Great Sports Rivalries
ISBN 979-8-8873-5947-2 (hard cover)
ISBN 979-8-8873-5986-1 (paperback)
ISBN 979-8-8904-2045-9 (EPUB)
ISBN 979-8-8904-2104-3 (eBook)
Library of Congress Control Number: 2023912509

Printed in the United States of America.

Photographs/Shutterstock/Newscom: Cover: Darren Lee/Cal Sport Media, Robin Alam/Icon SportswireviaNewscom; p 5, 6, 9, 10, 13, 14, 17, 18, 21: EFKS; p 5: Larry Radloff/Icon Sportswire; p 6: Tom Lynn; p 9: Darren Lee; p 10: Kirsten Schmitt; p 13: Brian Kersey; p 14: John Biever/Icon SMI; p 17: Mark Black; p 18: John J. Kim; p 20: Larry Radloff/Icon Sportswire; p 21: Rich Sugg

Seahorse Publishing Company

www.seahorsepub.com

Published in the United States
Seahorse Publishing
PO Box 771325
Coral Springs, FL 33077